Savor THE Savior

Pen, Bible, Ice Cream!

Advantage™
INSPIRATIONAL

Jeri R. Daniel

Savor the Savior by Jeri R. Daniel
Copyright © 2011 by Jeri R. Daniel
All Rights Reserved.
ISBN 13: 978-1-59755-264-6

Published by: ADVANTAGE BOOKS™
www.advbookstore.com

This book and parts thereof may not be reproduced in any form, stored in a retrieval system or transmitted in any form by any means (electronic, mechanical, photocopy, recording or otherwise) without prior written permission of the author, except as provided by United States of America copyright law.

Scripture taken from the HOLY BIBLE, NEW INTERNATIONAL VERSION®. Copyright © 1973, 1978, 1984 Biblica. Used by permission of Zondervan. All rights reserved. The "NIV" and "New International Version" trademarks are registered in the United States Patent and Trademark Office by Biblica. Use of either trademark requires the permission of Biblica.

Library of Congress Control Number: 2011928980

Cover design by Pat Theriault

First Printing: July 2011
11 12 13 14 15 16 17   10 9 8 7 6 5 4 3 2 1
Printed in the United States of America

Dedication

This book is dedicated to my One True Love, Jesus, and to my one true love, Ron. I'm so glad we were all brought together!

Jeri Daniel

Endorsements

"Every growing child of God wants to worship and praise their Lord. Problem is most of us don't know how to worship the Lord. In this little book, Jeri Daniel not only teaches us how to worship God through journaling, but she also gives us scores of illustrations. *Savor the Savior* is packed with simple, easy to follow, practical instruction for developing your own personal love language for God. Your quiet time will never be the same as she challenges all of us to go deeper in our personal relationship to Jesus. This isn't a 'read it and sit it on the shelf' book. It's a how-to guide for keeping your first love for Christ as hot as the day you were saved!"
    Rick Ray
    Executive Pastor
    First Baptist Oviedo, FL

"The easiest way to make a new friend is to be with a friend who introduces you. Jeri Daniel is the friend who guides you with her book *Savor the Savior* into a deep friendship with Jesus. In simple, enjoyable steps Jeri leads you with pen and paper to using the scriptures to discover the Savior. It's like sitting down over tea or lunch and being introduced to someone in such a way that you are sure a friendship will develop. And then Jeri will quietly slip away and leave you to your own intimate relationship, with your friend, Jesus. Excellent book! I can see it being a blessing to many! I endorse it wholeheartedly!"
    Pastor Jim DeVore
    Cornerstone Church of Littlerock, CA

"Ice cream quenches the taste buds like God's Word quenches the soul. This book is a step by step method on journaling your way to a closer relationship with Christ. Not only do I have the pleasure of calling Jeri "friend," I am also her neighbor. I get to see the benefits of this approach on a day to day basis. This book will leave you wanting to start journaling right away, with a huge bowl of your favorite ice cream." :)

Greg & Melanie Wilkinson
"Having a Ball with Greg & Mel"
www.GregandMel.org

Acknowledgments

I thank my Jesus, who led me to give this book back to Him through my church, First Baptist Church of Oviedo. This is definitely a church made up of the people, not the building. "The Caring Place" sure lives up to its name!

I am forever grateful to each and every one who obeyed when prompted to speak the Truth to me at any given time in my life. You know who you are. Thanks to all who encouraged me to follow through with "the book."

Amy, Lisa, Kara, Angie, Lydia, and Kaleb, I am incredibly thankful to be your Mama. You are so deeply loved! Thank you for your understanding when I was bleary eyed from working on this in the middle of the night.

Ron Daniel, what a capacity you have to love your family! Thank you for choosing us so faithfully. You really are my best friend.

Thank you to Alex and Jill Moen, along with Melba and Dave Daniel, for setting me up with my hubby and pointing me to Christ.

Mom, (Nana, Bebe) what would I do without your constant encouragement! The longer I know you, the more beautiful you are! Thank you for going the second mile so very often.

Jeri Daniel

I greatly appreciate the editing help from each of you who cheered me on with honesty: Don and Cory Freeman, Jena Stephans, Jodi Worrall, Bebe Seabolt, Darren and Karen Hunt, Deb McCrary, and Doug and Darlene Peters.

Bruster's Real Ice Cream in Oviedo, I am so grateful for the 100 free ice cream donations.

Table of Contents

SECTION ONE - SUMMARY/OVERVIEW 11

SECTION TWO - INTRODUCTION 13

SECTION THREE - THE METHOD 19
   Pray
   Underline
   Circle
   Write
   Read
   Add
   Close

SECTION FOUR - QUESTIONS AND ANSWERS 30

SECTION FIVE - ENCOURAGEMENT 34

SECTION SIX - APPENDIX 36
   Samples for all levels

SECTION SEVEN - TEACHER'S GUIDE 60
   Before Day One
   Day One
   Day Two
   Day Three
   Day Four
   Teacher's Closure

Jeri Daniel

SECTION ONE

SUMMARY/OVERVIEW

What's the point?

Savor the Savior will teach you how to pick out your favorite morsels of Scripture, savor each one, and praise the Lord, who lovingly prepared them. *Like spooning through your favorite ice cream, searching for the swirls and chunks of extra special rewards hiding within, you will discover an amazingly simple method for studying the Bible.* Expect your prayer life to strengthen and be prepared to develop an ever deepening love for the One Who truly loves you, Jesus Christ. The bulletized reminder steps for this technique will become second nature after just a few uses, and the tools will last you a lifetime. Keeping a written journal record of your relationship with God will reveal where He has led in the past, increase your present faith, and continue to guide you in the future. Bon appétit! Enjoy!

Jeri Daniel

SECTION TWO

INTRODUCTION

Who is He...this *True* Love?

I "prayed the prayer" to ask God to forgive me for my sins, thanked Him, and acknowledged my belief that Jesus and God are the same person. Unfortunately, I was missing a most valuable piece of information. For the following three years I struggled in the quick sand of my own sins, thinking that I was capable of pulling myself to freedom from them, but instead sinking further down into the muck. I ached to feel *true* love, but felt unworthy. After dishonest relationships and seeking to fill my own need for love and acceptance, I finally found a Christian man. He actually accepted me, even after I revealed to him every past failure I could remotely recall. He was willing to walk with me together toward God, and we were to be married the following year.

One Sunday morning, I finally found the missing link. I sat with my future husband and with my pastor as I prepared to be baptized by immersion. I had already been baptized by sprinkling at a previous church, but I knew I had not been right with God at that time. To me, *this* baptism was supposed to be a symbol of my promise to God that I would try *even harder* to live as I knew He wanted me to. Besides, I needed to be baptized by immersion in order to join my fiancée's church, where we were planning to be married in only a few months.

During the traditional conversation which was routine before the baptism, the pastor asked me the age old question, "If you were to stand at the gates of Heaven today, and were asked why you should be allowed in, what would you say?" Well... hmmm... I hadn't ever thought of it like that before... well... hmmm...??? Because... well... hmmm... because...I have *really tried* to be good." *"God, You know how hard I've been trying, don't You? That counts, right?"* As I glanced up and saw the eyes of my poor fiancée turn to saucers, I pretty much guessed that I had gotten *that* answer wrong. The pastor cleared his throat and all but elbowed my hubby-to-be in the ribs so he would catch his jaw from hitting the floor. Would I lose him now?

As I listened to the pastor's explanation, I suddenly realized that I had been struggling so hard to do something that had already been done for me long ago. Christ had already paid the price of *all* my sins. It was finished. What a relief! I was so thankful to know that I was not responsible for earning my way to Heaven! My response that day was with absolute understanding, deepest gratitude, and a peaceable relief. My motivation for baptism was no longer distorted. To be baptized was a picture of all of those sins (that quick sand) being washed away from me. I was now free to walk with my Lord and serve Him in response to my utmost appreciation. I was just beginning to understand how much I was adored by the One who made me. He valued me enough to give His only Son in my place so that I could live with Him forever. My search for love was finally over. Jesus Christ *had* to be my One *True* Love!

But, there's only so much I can say!

In response to this amazing love shown to me, I dedicated my life to the Lord. I was eager to find out as much as I could about this new Love of my life. Shortly after my husband and I were married, I joined an in-depth Bible study to try to make some sense of the Scriptures, which had always been a struggle for me to understand.

> *...but God has revealed it to us by his Spirit. The Spirit searches all things, even the deep things of God. For who among men knows the thoughts of a man except the man's spirit within him? In the same way no one knows the thoughts of God except the Spirit of God. We have not received the spirit of the world but the Spirit who is from God, that we may understand what God has freely given us. This is what we speak, not in words taught us by human wisdom but in words taught by the Spirit, expressing spiritual truths in spiritual words. The man without the Spirit does not accept the things that come from the Spirit of God, for they are foolishness to him, and he cannot understand them, because they are spiritually discerned.*
> 1 Corinthians 2:10-14

Words that I had read before, which used to cause confusion, now spoke directly to me. I was hungry for more. I began to read a chapter every night, determined to read through the whole Bible. Though there were still portions that overwhelmed me, I was starting to see how it all went together.

At the conclusion of the Bible study class we were to spend three hours in a room at the church all alone with God for a time of prayer and meditation. *I began to freak out.* Three hours??? Praying??? My husband had lovingly told me before that I had the "gift of gab"...but to talk for three hours??? To God??? What could I possibly say???

I figured that I would make a list of everything I could think of to tell God thank you for...that should take at least...half an hour...

I could sing...*no, people might hear me.* Well, I could sing in my head. God would hear that, and that would be like praying. I knew lots of Christian songs...that should take another...half an hour...

Surely I could use up another half an hour asking God to bless and heal people I knew. This still left me with another hour and a half.

In the end, I struggled through what was supposed to be a special time with God. I think I ended up dozing off somewhere at the two and a half hours mark.

I wish I had known then what I know now!

How can I study the Bible *on my own*?

Over the next several years I took many different types of formal Bible Study classes and read through various daily devotionals. Despite the fact that they all helped me to grow in my relationship with Christ, there was a recurring problem: Each and every time that I was left unaided by a book or a class, I slipped into a dry spell. I was dependent on the accountability that came from participation in a group setting, and relied upon the "spoon-feeding" of specific questions to accompany a given Bible reading. I still especially favored reading through a Bible chapter at one sitting, because I often misunderstood verses used out of context. I struggled, however, with the consistency and quality of my relationship with God. Though I was *hearing*, I wasn't very good at *listening* to what He was saying to me. At this point I had yet to discover the difference between thanking Him and praising Him.

Getting from there to here

Every once in a while, one of the Bible study questions or assignments would instruct us to take a particular verse and personalize it, substituting our own name or personal pronoun where appropriate. I always detested these questions. *What a waste of time!* Why bother rewriting what is supposed to be perfect already? After all, it's Scripture. Isn't rewriting it sacrilegious or something anyway? When I reluctantly, but obediently, followed through, I started to really hear God speaking to me....not in an audible voice....but in a way that I sensed His close presence. I began to realize that He truly speaks *to me* when I carefully read His Word.

Have you ever made or received a phone call and spoken in a friendly voice to the person on the other end only to discover that the "person" was really a recording? Some of these are so realistic that it takes a few attempts to be absolutely sure it is not a human being. Once assured that it is a generalized message and not a living, breathing person talking to us individually, we tune it out, hurry past it, or hang up. Reading God's Word as a general message was a struggle for me to receive in a personal way. I knew the importance of reading my Bible, and I *was* learning, but I was missing the relational part of the communication.

This personalizing technique of writing love letters to God has shown me how much of His Word truly is uniquely and specifically chosen *just* for me each and every time that I meet with Him. Before long I began applying the method to larger sections of Scripture and recording it in my daily journal entries. It eventually developed into a complete system of journal writing, which I will take you through step by step in this book. Whether you start out simply with a Bible verse or two, or you dive in head first studying a full chapter each day, you will immediately see God in a whole new light. His message is *just* for you, too!

Jeri Daniel

SECTION THREE

THE METHOD

How to write a letter of adoration to the One whom adores you the most: your *True* Love

"On your mark..."

Materials list

I use the cheapest **composition notebook** that I can find. They are easy to locate. Most drugstores and grocery stores carry them (and sometimes the dollar stores, too). I prefer to use an **ink pen**. Pencil just doesn't show up well enough for my liking, and since I mark my Bible with the same writing instrument, I don't want to use markers or gel pens which easily bleed through those thin pages. Though I do not always do this, I like to alternate between blue and black ink for each different day. At a later date, when I read through the journal, it makes for much easier readability. I use a **study Bible**, which especially helps with some historical or language obscurities that I run across. It provides the immediate convenience of study helps on the same page in my Bible that I am already reading. *Important: Choose a Bible that you are comfortable writing in.* A **Bible dictionary**, though bulky, will do the same as a study Bible and is worth the price to have as a reference tool for years to come. Keep everything together for easy daily access in your special "spot" for quiet time with God.

The efficiency of set up and clean up often determines the quality and quantity of your time away with your True Love.

Pray that God will speak to you through His Word.

But when he, the Spirit of truth, comes, he will guide you into all truth. He will not speak on his own; he will speak only what he hears, and he will tell you what is yet to come. John 16:13

Pick a chapter, any chapter.

All Scripture is God-breathed and is useful for teaching, rebuking, correcting and training in righteousness, so that the man of God may be thoroughly equipped for every good work.
2 Timothy 3:16-17

To put into practice this method for praising God, it is generally easier to start with a Psalm that is already praising Him, but *any Scripture can be used.* Even those verses that tell all of the "begats" tell us something about our True Love. You may start out with a verse or two until you get the hang of it, but gradually try more when you can. I prefer to read through one chapter each day, moving through a complete book of the Bible before choosing another that I feel led to study. Some Scripture blossoms into a lengthy letter. Some Scripture remains a tiny bud of affection. There is no wrong way.

What does this have to do with *me*?
This is the question that needs to be in your mind while reading the Scripture.

So is my word that goes out from my mouth: It will not return to me empty, but will accomplish what I desire and achieve the purpose for which I sent it.
Isaiah 55:11

It is personal from God to you. Why is God telling you what He is telling you? Just think about it as you read.

"Get set..."

Graffiti is okay here. Mark it up.

Underline *everything* that you recognize as *personal communication* from God to you as you read through the passage the first time. (Think of these as the swirls in that favorite ice cream.) Circle parts that are especially meaningful. (These would be the chunks in the ice cream.) It may be a glimpse of His character, or a message of what He has done or what He wants you to do. It could be what He thinks of you. It may be an acknowledgement of a promise made or kept. Don't miss anything that speaks to you, but do not feel you must mark everything. There are often large sections of Scripture that I just do not recognize as personal communication from God to me. This doesn't mean it is useless, only that it does not apply to this particular time of praise. *NOTE: If you do not understand a term or reference, this is when you look it up in a study Bible or a Bible Dictionary.*

Finding His Features

These definitions help me to realize that I am not just hunting down items for a "thank you" card for my "ice cream." I am acknowledging the true person of God. Notice how these words help to define each other. Use them to search for every detail of the Lord in the Scripture.

***Distinctive* –**
Uniquely *characteristic* of a particular person, group, or thing

***Quality* –**
A *distinctive characteristic* of somebody or something

***Recognizable* –**
To identify a thing or person because of having perceived him, her, or it before

***Characteristic* –**
A feature or *quality* that makes somebody or something *recognizable*

***Attribute* –**
A *quality*, property, or *characteristic* of somebody or something

What do I already know about my True Love?

Which of His features do I recognize?

Reminisce.
If you see someone you know well from a distance, you may recognize him by his particular walk or by the distinct sound of his voice or maybe by his mannerisms. You may recognize the work that someone has done just by what you know previously of his character. You already know *something* about God, even if you are a brand new Christian. He saved you, right? He sacrificed His Son for you, right? He created the universe, judges fairly, and keeps His promises. What kind of "person" does those things? The longer you have known Him and the more time you have spent with Him, the more you will recognize Him throughout

Scripture. Sometimes as you read through a passage, it may seem as if He is hiding with only a glimpse revealed, but you will sense His familiarity as you walk with Him daily and are filled with His Holy Spirit to guide you.

The Dual: Thankfulness versus Adoration
Though both thankfulness and adoration are important, they are not interchangeable. Thankfulness acknowledges what God does. Adoration tells who He is, which is made known to us by what He says and does. Here are four examples:

T - Thank you for answering my prayers.
A - You are such a generous God. You are always faithful to keep Your promises. I can trust in You for all things. You are the Father Who gives to His child out of love.

T - Thank you for loving me.
A - You are full of grace and mercy. You love me in spite of my daily shortcomings. I love You with all my heart, mind, and soul because You first loved me. I am all Yours.

T - Thank you for helping me.
A - You will never leave me nor forsake me. You are my help, my comforter, my counselor, my wisdom, and my strength. I never need to worry or fear, because You are always with me and work all things together for good to those who love you.

T - Thank you for my family.
A - You have given me the desires of my heart in the gift of my family. You reward us when we delight in You. Your plan is perfect. Your timing is right. You love my loved ones even more than I do. I can trust them to You.

Who am I talking to, anyway?

When I write a letter to a loved one, I say, "I love *you.*" I wouldn't use he/she/him/her. In this type of journaling you are speaking directly *to* God, not *about* Him. Write the letter *to Him,* telling Him *who He is to you and who you are to him. Give the reasons why.*

"Go!"

Begin.

I include the date and the Scripture at the top of my journal page. I like to use all caps for the word, "SCRIPTURE" so it is easy to locate later when I read back through it. Since I use the same notebook for sermon notes and prayer requests, I also write "Journal" as the title, again for easy distinction later. (See Section Six Sample One)

Plagiarism is okay.

Referring to all of the underlined portions of Scripture, start writing what you see of God. Tell Him what you recognize. If you like the wording the way it is in the Scripture, simply copy it. Be sure to use personal pronouns (I, me, my, mine) in the appropriate places. If the Scripture in a section is something that seems confusing to you because of the wording, simply reword it in a way that is comfortable and natural for you.

Use shortcuts.

Abbreviate everything that you can as you write, in order to maintain the flow of your thoughts (b/c = because, w/ = with, & = and, etc.) Write your codes inside the journal cover.

Don't look back until you reach the finish line.
Continue this throughout the entire portion of Scripture you have chosen for the day. *CAUTION: Do not stop and read what you have written, yet. Take one more step.*

Get real.
As you go, you will be prompted to acknowledge other things that may not be directly referred to in the verse you are on. Go ahead and write them down. Make it personal.

Stop.

Rewind and play it again.
Now, read what you just wrote from beginning to end. Isn't it amazing? You have just written some beautiful stuff!

What else?
Often times, after reading through that first bit, you will feel prompted to tell Him one more thing....or more; so, do it. Come on...don't hold anything back! He already knows what you're thinking anyway. You might as well just put it in writing.

Humble yourself before the Lord.

Find the differences.

> *But he gives us more grace. That is why Scripture says: "God opposes the proud but gives grace to the humble."* James 4:6

Remember those picture games where you are supposed to find the differences between two similar pictures? We are made in God's image, so there are some similarities, but there sure are a whole lot of things wrong when we compare who we are to who God is! List them, and be prepared to receive His grace.

...For when I am weak, then I am strong...
2 Corinthians 12:10b

In light of what I've just acknowledged about God, I am many times in awe at the comparison between Him and myself. I am weak; He is strong. Ask yourself, "What is it about Him that I love so much more than what I love about myself?"

Fess up.
Okay, so I said it was a love letter, not an apology letter. When moved by immense love for another, it naturally comes into play to make *right* anything that is *not already right* between you, *right*? So *admit* your faults, mistakes...yes, admit your sins to God.

Wash up.
Ask for *forgiveness* for all areas of self-focus...yes, we're talking about those sins again.

Fill up.
If we are full of ourselves, there is not room to be full of the Spirit. Now that we've been emptied of "self" by confessing our mess-ups and asking for forgiveness for them, we can truly be filled....and why not go the extra bit, and ask for "overflowing!" Pray that God will fill you to *overflowing* with His Holy Spirit. How else can we expect to change? He is our Comforter, Counselor, our Guide, our access to God's Wisdom and Power. He is Jesus within us.

Express your appreciation.
Now is the time to say, "Thank you." Typically, this is not a huge section of the letter for me. Simply stated, I am thankful for answered prayers, abundant blessings, salvation, His presence, His promises, His Word. If I have specific answered prayers, I may list them here, or I may write them instead in the margin next to the original request...which may even be in a previous journal notebook. My "silent" (unwritten) prayers tend to have the bulk of my thankfulness within them.

Give what you have to offer.

Therefore, I urge you, brothers, in view of God's mercy, to offer your bodies as living sacrifices, holy and pleasing to God—this is your spiritual act of worship. Romans 12:1

I am under vows to you, O God; I will present my thank offerings to you. Psalm 56:12

"Promises, promises, you can't keep." Don't let this be said of you. As you study the Bible you will come to see the value of a vow or promise between you and God. Do *not* take it lightly. Because we are imperfect, you may need to sacrifice the same things daily: yourself, your day, your loved ones, and your burdens.

Not my will.

Going a little farther, he fell with his face to the ground and prayed, "My Father, if it is possible, may this cup be taken from me. Yet not as I will, but as you will." Matthew 26:39

Follow His example. Jesus made His request known, but above all, He asked for God's will.

Pray for God's *perfect* will to be done.

I know that you can do all things; no plan of yours can be thwarted. Job 42:2

(NOTE: Thwart means "to prevent somebody or somebody's plan from being successful.")

Did you get that? His plan *is* going to be successful. But because He allows us to have *free will*, His *perfect* will is not always done. Wouldn't you rather things go *perfectly* according to His plan? Do you really trust Him? Tell Him so, and prove it by allowing Him to be in control of *every* aspect of your life each day.

What is A.C.T.S?

A.C.T.S. is a common guideline for prayer, and it stands for: Adoration, Confession, Thanksgiving, and Supplication. The method described in this book includes the first three, with the focus on Adoration. You may choose to place the letters "A," "C," "T," before each corresponding section of your love letter journal entry.

Sign it…or "Amen."

Signing your letter is optional, but after all, it *is* a love letter. Another option is to end with "Amen," since it *is* also a prayer.

Whoa…what happened to the "S"?

My husband does pretty well with a "Honey-Do List" (the around-the-house-fix-it-wish-list a wife sometimes gives to her husband). He is *especially* sweet about it when he is feeling adored by me, but I wouldn't *think* of attaching a "Honey-Do List" to a love letter to him. Likewise, though the Supplication or Prayer Request section is Scriptural and *very* important, I suggest that you write it separately on the journal page after your "Love Letter" is complete. This keeps the focus on God *first*.

For the sake of time and convenience, I recommend having an ongoing prayer list (OPL) on a separate sheet of paper to be kept with the journal book. Updates and answered prayers may be noted in a love letter or on the OPL, which also serves as a bookmark. If your journal has space inside the front cover, you may also list general prayer topics according to the days of the week. Composition journals are ideal for this. In the "S" or Supplication section *after* the love letter, you may write, "OPL," as well as anything that is especially heavy on your heart.

Rewind for the encore.

Read what you have written again from beginning to end. It will be far from a fine piece of literature, but it will be yours and His. Full of praise, isn't it? Doesn't it just make you love Him that much more?!

Conclusion

You did it! Read these verses about spiritual growth and maturity:

> *Anyone who lives on milk, being still an infant, is not acquainted with the teaching about righteousness. But solid food is for the mature, who by constant use have trained themselves to distinguish good from evil.*
> Hebrews 5:13-14

> *Taste and see that the LORD is good; blessed is the man who takes refuge in him.* Psalm 34:8

May you move from living on "milk" to digesting the "solid food" of His Word each and every day. *Taste and see that the Lord is good!* **Savor the Savior!**

SECTION FOUR

QUESTIONS AND ANSWERS

Q: Should I journal *every* day?
A: Aim for a *quiet time* with God *every* day. On some days it is not realistic to write very much, if anything at all. On those days, simply note: the *date*, the *Scripture* read, *silent prayers* to acknowledge unwritten prayer time, and *OPL* to refer to the separate prayer request list. Another option is to list only the words that you circled as your very favorite "nuggets" (See Section Six Sample Five). This record of your quiet time will show you the quantity and quality that you are investing in your relationship with God. Your True Love desires time with you *every* day and throughout each day. Don't throw in the towel if it seems like too much. Do what you can. He will honor your mutual desire to spend time with Him.

Q: Do quiet times *have* to be in the morning?
A: Nope! There was a time when I could not control my eyes from rolling to the back of my head at the mention of mornings for quiet times. I was NOT a morning person and loathed anyone who threatened to even come close to changing this. Throughout the years though, I have meandered through every hour of the day (and night) as a favorite quiet time. Pick a time that *regularly* works for you the best that you can: before work, after everyone else is in bed, before everyone else is up, during a routine time in

the afternoon, when your kiddos are napping, on your lunch break, in the middle of the night while dealing with insomnia or feeding a newborn. Your True Love will faithfully meet with you *every* chance that He can.

Q: How *long* is this going to take?
A: As little or as long as you choose. In the beginning I watched the clock because I was a little uncomfortable in this new relationship, and *honestly* there were other things that I would rather do than write. Now, I sometimes have to set a timer to make myself break away. The more time that you spend with someone, the more you get to know them and either like or dislike what you get to know. When it is someone you truly love, that time leads to a deeper love and a stronger desire to spend even more time together. *I can promise you this: You will **never** regret having spent "too much time" with your True Love.*

Q: What if it is *too* hard for me?
A: Keep it simple. Just write what is on your heart. After reading the Scripture, answer this question: *What do I love about God?*

Q: I don't like to write. Could I just *type* something on my computer instead?
A: Sure! I tried this for a couple of months and it worked fine. I prefer to write because my computer does not have the cozy atmosphere that I enjoy in my much loved chair by my favorite table and lamp.

Q: Do you just write all of this stuff down, or do you *say* any of these as a prayer?
A: I begin with an "opening" prayer on my knees speaking directly to God. When I read what I write (in my comfy chair) I

am reading it *to* Him. **Again, there is no wrong way. This is your own personal time with your True Love. If you have prayed to be filled with the Spirit, know that He *will* guide you.**

Q: **Is this the only way to study the Bible on my own?**
A: **Absolutely not!** There are many excellent resources to help you to dig deeper in other ways. This way is just my personal favorite, because it has worked for me consistently for so many years.

Q: **Is it okay to eat my meal while doing this?**
A: **It is completely up to you.** Feast with God, or "fast and pray," eating after you are done.

Q: **Is there another way to remember the steps, other than the Table of Contents?**
A: **Here you go!**

- **Pray:** Confession, filling, thanks, ongoing list of requests, and understanding of God's Word by the Holy Spirit.
- **Read** chosen Scripture for the day, **underlining** only what speaks to you personally. *(the swirls in the ice cream)*
- **Skim** through the *underlined parts*, **circling** favorite words, phrases, or those words which describe God. *(the chunks in the ice cream)*
- **Write your response *to God*** as a brief prayer letter using the circled parts and optionally the underlined parts.
- **Read** over what you wrote. **Add** any additional comments or requests that come to mind.
- **Close** in prayer.

Jeri Daniel

SECTION FIVE

ENCOURAGEMENT

My prayer for you

For this reason I kneel before the Father, from whom his whole family in heaven and on earth derives its name. I pray that out of his glorious riches he may strengthen you with power through his Spirit in your inner being, so that Christ may dwell in your hearts through faith. And I pray that you, being rooted and established in love, may have power, together with all the saints, to grasp how wide and long and high and deep is the love of Christ, and to know this love that surpasses knowledge—that you may be filled to the measure of all the fullness of God. Now to him who is able to do immeasurably more than all we ask or imagine, according to his power that is at work within us, to him be glory in the church and in Christ Jesus throughout all generations, for ever and ever! Amen.
Ephesians 3:14-21

Jeri Daniel

Savor the Savior

SECTION SIX

APPENDIX (SAMPLES)

Sample Love Letters and Journal Entries

Note: <u>Underlined</u> "swirls" of Scripture are also <u>underlined</u> in the samples, while **circled** "chunks" of Scripture are represented by **bold** print. All journal portions include the abbreviations mentioned earlier (& = and, b/c = because, w/ = with).

Jeri Daniel

SAMPLE ONE – Journal sample page

Note: This is just an outline example. Experiment with what works well for you. You may only write what is in bold, or include as much as you want.

(Date)   ***Journal***

Opening Prayer
(I may also list prayers with my husband or silent prayers here.)

OPL *(Ongoing Prayer Lists) OPL refers to all request lists which are read and prayed over: topical prayers listed by each day of the week inside the journal cover, as well as emailed requests, and a page to which specific requests are added regularly. This page is used as a bookmark in the journal. Experiment, and use what works for you.*
SCRIPTURE – **Psalm 37:4 (& notes from study Bible)**

A – (Adoration/Application from the Scripture read)
"I love You, because…"

C – (Confession)
"Please forgive me for…"

T – (Thanksgiving)
"Thank You for…"

S – (Supplication)
"I ask You for…"

Add optional additional comments, updates to prayer requests, etc.

SAMPLE TWO - Psalm 37:4

Short letter from one verse of Scripture

*<u>**Delight** yourself in the **Lord**, and He will **give you** the **desires of your heart.**</u>*
--Psalm 37:4

A – Lord, You want me to delight myself in You. This is ongoing. When I do, You give me the desires of my heart. You place the desires in my heart that You have planned for me, and then You satisfy those desires.

I love You, Father! I do find pleasure in You. So many times You have given me the desires of my heart. You answer prayers so faithfully. You are a Promise Keeper. You are my Everything!

C – Lord God, please forgive me for ever straying from You in any way, not delighting myself in You. Cleanse me and fill me with Your perfect Holy Spirit, giving me Your desires in my heart.

T – Thank You, Lord, for overwhelming blessings in my life.

Jeri Daniel

SAMPLE THREE - Psalm 27
Long length letter from medium length of Scripture

Note: The verse by verse details are included on this sample only, to clearly show where I formed each piece of my letter. It is repeated below as it would appear in my journal.

> *¹ The **LORD** is my **light** and my **salvation**— whom shall I fear? The LORD is the **stronghold of my life**—of whom shall I be afraid?*

You, Lord, are my Light & my salvation & the strength of my life. You deliver me from fear...

> *² When evil men advance against me to devour my flesh, when my enemies and my foes attack me, they will stumble and fall.*

...& from the enemies in my life (fears, temptations, sin).

> *³ Though an army besiege me, my heart will not fear; though war break out against me, even then will I be **confident.***

I am confident in You.

> *⁴ One thing I ask of the LORD, this is what I seek: that **I may dwell in the house of the LORD all the days of my life, to gaze upon the beauty of the LORD** and to seek him in his temple.*

You give me the desires of my heart. I want to live in Your presence all the days of my life. I will gaze upon Your beauty, Lord.

*⁵ For <u>in the day of trouble he will **keep me safe** in his dwelling; he will **hide me in** the **shelter** of his tabernacle and set me high upon a rock.</u>*

In times of trouble You keep me safe & hide me in Your presence.

*⁶ <u>Then my head will be exalted above the enemies who surround me; at his tabernacle will **I sacrifice with shouts of joy;** **I will sing and make music to the LORD.**</u>*

My head will be high above my enemies (fears, temptations, sin) all around me. I will offer sacrifices of joy in Your presence. (What will I give up for You? Show me if there is more to sacrifice right now.) I will sing praises to You, Lord.

⁷ <u>Hear my voice when I call, O LORD; be merciful to me and answer me.</u>

You hear my voice when I call! You are merciful to me, & You answer me.

*⁸ <u>My heart says of you, "Seek his face!" **Your face, LORD, I will seek.**</u>*

Lord, in my heart I seek Your face.

*⁹ Do not hide your face from me, do not turn your **servant** away in anger; you have been **my helper**. Do not reject me or forsake me, O God my Savior.*

Do not hide Your face from me. Do not turn me away in anger. I am Your servant. You have been my helper. Do not leave me nor forsake me, O God my Savior.

¹⁰ Though my father and mother forsake me, the LORD will receive me.

You accept me & take care of me, Lord, no matter what.

*¹¹ **Teach me** your way, O LORD; **lead me in a straight path** because of my oppressors.*

Teach me Your way, O Lord, & lead me in a straight path, b/c of my enemies (fears, temptations, sin).

¹² Do not turn me over to the desire of my foes, for false witnesses rise up against me, breathing out violence.

Don't give up on me.

*¹³ I am still **confident** of this: **I will see the goodness of the LORD** in the land of the living.*

I am confident that I will continue to see Your goodness, Lord.

*¹⁴ **Wait for the LORD; be strong and take heart and wait for the LORD.***

I will wait on You with strength & comfort, Lord!

My Love Letter based on Psalm 27 with A, C, T labels for Adoration, Confession, and Thanksgiving

A - You, Lord, are my Light & my salvation & the strength of my life. You deliver me from fear & from the enemies in my life (fears, temptations, sin). I am confident in You. You give me the desires of my heart. I want to live in Your presence all the days of my life. I will gaze upon Your beauty, Lord. In times of trouble You keep me safe & hide me in Your presence. My head will be high above my enemies (fears, temptations, sin) all around me. I will offer sacrifices of joy in Your presence. (What will I give up for You? Show me if there is more to sacrifice right now.) I will sing praises to You, Lord. You hear my voice when I call! You are merciful to me, & You answer me. Lord, in my heart, I seek Your face. Do not hide Your face from me. Do not turn me away in anger. I am Your servant. You have been my helper. Do not leave me nor forsake me, O God my Savior. You accept me & take care of me, Lord, no matter what. Teach me Your way, O Lord, & lead me in a straight path, b/c of my enemies (fears, temptations, sin). Don't give up on me. I am confident that I will continue to see Your goodness, Lord. I will wait on You with strength & comfort, Lord!

Additional adoration after reading through what was written on Psalm 27

Lord, You are so real & personable, so close to me in fellowship & yet God on high. I am greatly humbled at the abounding measures of Your grace, mercy, & love toward me: a "nobody" to most the world, but a princess in Your eyes. You made me just as You planned, & although I took so long to finally call out to You & give myself to You, & though I stumble daily in my attempts to walk on Your straight & narrow path, You love me endlessly & shower me w/ that affection. I love You, Lord w/ all that I am! Forever I am Yours, Lord.

C - Please forgive me for neglecting to recognize answered prayers. Please forgive me for self love over You & others. Please forgive my angry attitudes & words when I'm stressed. Please forgive me for embracing stress when I should be turning & clinging to You, Lord God. Please cleanse me & purify me, Father. Prepare me for Your plan. Fill me to overflowing. I am Yours, Lord! Use me for Your glory!

T – Thank You, God, for Your forgiveness. Thank You for abundant blessings: Your provision, protection, and presence. Thank You for answering prayers and keeping promises. Amen.

Jeri Daniel

SAMPLE FOUR - Joshua 10:1-15

Short length letter from medium length of Scripture, Old Testament

Note: This is a section of a chapter.

¹ Now Adoni-Zedek king of Jerusalem heard that Joshua had taken Ai and totally destroyed it, doing to Ai and its king as he had done to Jericho and its king, and that the people of Gibeon had made a treaty of peace with Israel and were living near them. ² He and his people were very much alarmed at this, because Gibeon was an important city, like one of the royal cities; it was larger than Ai, and all its men were good fighters. ³ So Adoni-Zedek king of Jerusalem appealed to Hoham king of Hebron, Piram king of Jarmuth, Japhia king of Lachish and Debir king of Eglon. ⁴ "Come up and help me attack Gibeon," he said, "because it has made peace with Joshua and the Israelites."
⁵ Then the five kings of the Amorites—the kings of Jerusalem, Hebron, Jarmuth, Lachish and Eglon—joined forces. They moved up with all their troops and took up positions against Gibeon and attacked it.
*⁶ The Gibeonites then sent word to Joshua in the camp at Gilgal: "**Do not abandon your servants. Come up to us quickly and save us! Help us**, because all the Amorite kings from the hill country have joined forces against us."*
⁷ So Joshua marched up from Gilgal with his entire army, including all the best fighting men. ⁸ The

LORD said _to Joshua,_ **_"Do not be afraid_** _of them; I have given them into your hand. Not one of them will be able to withstand you."_

⁹ _After an all-night march from Gilgal, Joshua took them by surprise._ ¹⁰ **_The LORD threw them into confusion_** _before Israel, who defeated them in a great victory at Gibeon. Israel pursued them along the road going up to Beth Horon and cut them down all the way to Azekah and Makkedah._ ¹¹ _As they fled before Israel on the road down from Beth Horon to Azekah,_ _the_ **_LORD hurled large hailstones_** _down on them from the sky, and more of them died from the hailstones than were killed by the swords of the Israelites._

¹² _On the day the LORD gave the Amorites over to Israel,_ **_Joshua said to the LORD_** _in the presence of Israel:_

    "**O sun, stand still** over Gibeon,
    O moon, over the Valley of Aijalon."
¹³ _**So the sun stood still,**_
    and the **moon stopped**,
    till the nation avenged itself on its enemies,
as it is written in the Book of Jashar.

The sun stopped in the middle of the sky and delayed going down about a full day. ¹⁴ _There has never been a day like it before or since,_ **_a day when the LORD listened to a man. Surely the LORD was fighting for Israel!_**

¹⁵ _Then Joshua returned with all Israel to the camp at Gilgal._

Savor the Savior

My Love Letter based on Joshua 10:1-15

A - Lord, You do not abandon Your servants. You come quickly to save and help. I need not fear b/c You will deliver me (through trials). You hear my prayers. You fight for Your people. You deliver my enemies into my hand (struggles w/ temptations). Lord, You will destroy all of my enemies against whom I fight (sins). You utterly destroy them. Your commands are perfect. You listen. You fight for Your children, and I am Your child.

C - Please forgive me for seeking comfort anywhere else, instead of running to You & filling up w/ Your Spirit. Please forgive me for doing first & praying later. Please forgive my fear in place of faith.

T - Thank You for Your deliverance, Your love, fresh starts, provision, guidance, protection, presence, overflowing blessings, loveable people in my life, comforts, health, salvation, & answered prayers. I love You, Lord!

Jeri Daniel

SAMPLE FIVE – Ephesians 4:29-5:2

List of the circled favorite "chunks" from medium length of Scripture, New Testament

Note: This abbreviated method is intended for short days, not to replace the full method entirely. Using the list of key words and phrases, pray silently as you feel led.

> ²⁹*Do not let any unwholesome* **talk** *come out of your mouths, but only what is* **helpful** *for* **building others up** *according to their needs, that it may* **benefit those who listen.** ³⁰*And do not grieve the* **Holy Spirit of God**, *with whom you were* **sealed** *for the day of* **redemption.** ³¹*Get rid of all bitterness, rage and anger, brawling and slander, along with every form of malice.* ³²*Be* **kind** *and* **compassionate** *to one another,* **forgiving** *each other, just as in* **Christ God forgave** *you.*
>
> ¹**Be imitators of God**, *therefore,* **as dearly loved children** ²*and* **live a life of love**, *just as* **Christ loved us** *and* **gave himself up for us** *as a* **fragrant offering** *and* **sacrifice to God**.

My Love List based on Ephesians 4:29 – 5:2

A – helpful talk, build others up, benefit listeners, Holy Spirit of God, sealed, redemption, kind, compassionate, forgiving, Christ God forgave, imitator of God as dearly loved child, live life of love, Christ loved us, gave himself, fragrant offering, sacrifice to God

C, T – **Silent prayers**

Jeri Daniel

SAMPLE SIX – Psalm 61

Short length letter from short length of Scripture, Psalms

*¹ **Hear my cry, O God;**
   listen to my prayer.*
*² From the ends of the earth **I call** to you,
   I call as my heart grows faint;
   lead me to the rock that is higher than I.*
*³ For you have been my **refuge**,
   a **strong tower** against the foe.*
*⁴ I long to **dwell** in your tent forever
   and take **refuge** in the **shelter** of your wings.
   Selah*
*⁵ For you have **heard my vows**, O God;
   you have given me the **heritage** of those who **fear your name**.*
*⁶ Increase the days of the king's life,
   his years for many generations.*
*⁷ May he be enthroned in God's presence forever;
   appoint your love and faithfulness to protect him.*
*⁸ Then will I ever **sing praise** to your name
   and **fulfill** my **vows** day after day.*

My Love Letter based on Psalm 61

A - God, You hear my cries & attend to my prayers. I know I can cry to You when my heart is overwhelmed. You lead me to safety. You have been a shelter for me, a strong tower from the enemy. I will stay w/ You forever! I will trust in the shelter of Your wings. (I will trust You to protect me.) You, O God, have heard my vows. You have given me the heritage of those who fear Your name. (I will enjoy living w/ You in Heaven forever!) I will sing praise to Your name forever, that I may daily perform my vows to stay w/ You, trust You, & praise You.

C - Lord, please forgive me for putting myself before others in any way. Please cleanse me from all sin. Fill me to overflowing w/ Your Holy Spirit.

T - Thank You for being in control of all things & for allowing circumstances which will draw us closer to You. Thank You for so many answered prayers! Thank You for time alone with you and for the privilege of being used by You. Thank You for blessing me so richly in so many ways: my nation, church family, extended family, husband, children, home, health, daily provisions, eternity with You.

May Your perfect will be done in every aspect of my life.

SAMPLE SEVEN – James 1

Medium length letter from medium length of Scripture, New Testament

^{1}*James, a servant of God and of the Lord Jesus Christ,*
To the twelve tribes scattered among the nations:
Greetings.
^{2}<u>*Consider it **pure joy**, my brothers, whenever you face trials of many kinds,*</u> ^{3}<u>*because you know that the testing of your faith develops perseverance.*</u> ^{4}<u>*Perseverance must finish its work so that you may be mature and complete, not lacking anything.*</u> ^{5}<u>*If any of you lacks wisdom, he should ask **God**, who **gives generously to all without finding fault**, and it will be given to him.*</u> ^{6}<u>*But when he asks, he must believe and not doubt,*</u> *because he who doubts is like a wave of the sea, blown and tossed by the wind.* ^{7}*That man should not think he will receive anything from the Lord;* ^{8}*he is a double-minded man, unstable in all he does.*
^{9}<u>*The brother in humble circumstances ought to take pride in his high position.*</u> ^{10}*But the one who is rich should take pride in his low position, because he will pass away like a wild flower.* ^{11}*For the sun rises with scorching heat and withers the plant; its blossom falls and its beauty is destroyed. In the same way, the rich man will fade away even while he goes about his business.*
^{12}<u>*Blessed is the man who perseveres under trial, because when he has stood the test, he will **receive***</u>

the crown of life that God has promised to those who love him. ¹³When tempted, no one should say, "God is tempting me." For God cannot be tempted by evil, nor does he tempt anyone; ¹⁴but each one is tempted when, by his own evil desire, he is dragged away and enticed. ¹⁵Then, after desire has conceived, it gives birth to sin; and sin, when it is full-grown, gives birth to death.

¹⁶Don't be deceived, my dear brothers. ¹⁷*Every good and perfect gift is from above, coming down from the Father of the heavenly lights, who does not change like shifting shadows.* ¹⁸He chose to give us birth through the word of truth, that we might be a kind of firstfruits of all he created.

¹⁹My dear brothers, take note of this: Everyone should be quick to listen, slow to speak and slow to become angry, ²⁰for man's anger does not bring about the **righteous life** that **God desires**. ²¹Therefore, get rid of all moral filth and the evil that is so prevalent and humbly accept the word planted in you, which can save you.

²²**Do not merely listen** to the word, and so deceive yourselves. **Do** what it says. ²³Anyone who listens to the word but does not do what it says is like a man who looks at his face in a mirror ²⁴and, after looking at himself, goes away and immediately forgets what he looks like. ²⁵But the man who looks intently into the **perfect law that gives freedom**, and continues to do this, not forgetting what he has heard, but doing it—he will be **blessed** in what he does.

*²⁶If anyone considers himself religious and yet does not <u>keep a tight rein on his tongue,</u> he deceives himself and his religion is worthless. ²⁷<u>Religion that God our Father</u> accepts as <u>**pure and faultless** is this: to **look after** orphans and widows in their distress and to keep oneself from being polluted by the world.</u>*

My Love Letter based on James 1

A - I can consider it pure joy in the midst of trials of many kinds, knowing that You are allowing my faith to be tested to develop perseverance to mature & complete me to the point that I am not lacking anything. If I am lacking wisdom, I only need to ask You, God. You give generously to all without finding fault, & You will give me wisdom when I ask. You expect my belief in You. You value humility. You bless those who persevere under trial with the crown of life that You have promised to those who love You. You cannot be tempted by evil, nor do you tempt anyone. Every good and perfect gift is from You above, Father of the heavenly lights. You do not change. You expect me to be quick to listen, slow to speak and slow to become angry, b/c my anger does not bring about the righteous life that You desire. You save me through the humble acceptance of the Word planted in me. You expect me to do what it says. If I look intently into the perfect law that gives freedom, and do not forget what I have heard, but do it, I will be blessed in what I do. You expect me to keep a tight rein on my tongue. Religion that You, God my Father, accept as pure and faultless is this: to look after orphans and widows in their distress and to keep myself from being polluted by the world.

Lord God, You work in mysterious ways, the opposite of the world around me. Your expectations are great, but so are your blessings and rewards. You are unchanging. You chose me. You are righteous. You want me to walk closely with You. I love You, Father.

C & S - Please forgive me for all forms of selfishness & complaining, & for letting other things get in front of my time with You. Cleanse me, please, God, and fill me fully with Your Spirit. Please give me the wisdom for all decisions I am currently struggling with and show me Your perfect will. My life is Yours. Please use me to bring many people close to You. May You receive all the glory forever. Amen.

Savor the Savior

SECTION SEVEN

TEACHER'S GUIDE

BEFORE DAY ONE

Fellowship fun...

You may have heard that the best way to learn is by involving as many of our senses as we can. These lessons are designed to do just that. Although anyone can read <u>Savor the Savior</u> independently and follow the steps right away, accountability is ideal to developing this daily routine as a habit. I've broken it down into four fun lessons for you with flexibility to do what will work for your particular group.

Since this study method is useful for all kinds of people, choose what will work with the age, stage, and gender of your group. Don't neglect the fun parts of the lesson for adult groups! They will enjoy the fellowship, too.

Here are some ideas for setting up the theme for the first class:

- Send out invitations. Be sure to include RSVP details, so you know how many books and supplies to order. Request prepayment if applicable. You may copy "What's the Point?" from the book for the invitation.
- Have everyone bring different ingredients for ice cream sundaes.
- Serve ice cream in waffle cones.

- Have one ice cream flavor with a combination of "swirls" and "chunks" in it. ("Moose Tracks" is my personal favorite!)
- Plan to go out for ice cream after the class. (Look for coupons beforehand.)
- Decorate the covers of composition notebooks with scrapbooking paper (maybe in an ice cream theme).
- Granted, everyone cannot eat ice cream, and maybe time will not allow for it. You may want to draw a simple picture of a dish or cone of ice cream on a white board or poster board. Be sure to include the "swirls" and "chunks."

Plan ahead...

Have students pre-buy the Savor the Savior books so they arrive before the first class. Also, buying the notebooks and pens ahead of time will ensure that each student has what is needed for the lesson.

Be sure every person has a Bible that they are willing to write in. If this is a concern, consider looking at the dollar store or even your local thrift store for extra Bibles. BibleGateway.com is a great resource for printing the Scripture passage that is needed for each lesson. You can then make copies to have available as a *backup* for those who do not have a Bible.

Do you remember the Materials List from Section Three?

Here it is again for each student:

- *A copy of the book, Savor the Savior*
- *One composition notebook*
- *One ink pen*
- *Bible that can be written in*

- *If it is not a Study Bible, a Bible dictionary can be shared by the group. (A regular dictionary will do in a pinch.)*

For the class, the teacher will also need a white board, dry erase markers (that work), and an eraser.

DAY ONE

Set up...

Before the students arrive, write the following journal entry onto the board:

(Date) Journal

- *Opening prayer*
- *Ongoing prayer list*
- *SCRIPTURE* – **Psalm 37:4**

Delight yourself in the Lord, and He will give you the desires of your heart.

Start with prayer...

Ask the Holy Spirit to guide the lesson and bring understanding. Pray that only the words which are meant to be spoken will be said, according to God's perfect will. Pray for the members of the group; God has each one there for a particular purpose. Pray that He will be glorified by the lesson.

Settle in...

While everyone is getting settled with their materials, and maybe while finishing their ice cream, ask the ice breaker question: ***What is your favorite ice cream and why?*** Don't rush through this first session. It's just the kick-off, so there will be plenty of time to complete the actual lesson. Take the time for everyone to get engaged as a class.

Subjects for prayers...

Composition notebooks often have spaces inside the front cover for students to list their class information by the day of the week. This is a great place to list basic prayer subjects, which can also be divided by the days of the week.

Here are some ideas to jot down, but take a minute to brainstorm as a class (use abbreviations whenever possible):

Sunday – worldwide church, persecuted, missions, ministries, church leaders and their families
Monday - salvations, health, relationships, marriages, family, friends, neighbors, all contacts, jobs/provisions
Tuesday - government, nation, world, troops
Wednesday - victims, lonely, those suffering a loss, marriages
Thursday - imprisoned, addicts, poor
Friday - emailed requests, jobless, provision
Saturday - stewardship, orderliness, scheduling, parenting, schooling, wisdom/future/decisions, etc.

The list is helpful to jog your memory, so that each day you can focus on a group of requests that go together. Specific requests, updates, and answered prayers may be listed throughout the journal as you feel led. (I love to use the margins for these.)

Super easy seatwork...

Students should copy the sample journal entry and Psalm 37:4 from the white board onto their first journal page.

Savor the Savior together...

The group will read all of Section One, "What's the Point?" together. Have a different person read each sentence. Challenge the group to make it flow as if only one person is reading it.

Tune in to teacher-talk...

Teacher, read this aloud to the class:

What does this have to do with *me*? This is the question that needs to be in your mind while reading the Scripture.

so is my word that goes out from my mouth: It will not return to me empty, but will accomplish what I desire and achieve the purpose for which I sent it.
Isaiah 55:11

It is personal from God to you. Why is God telling you what He is telling you? Just think about it as you read.

Have a volunteer read Psalm 37:4 from the journal entry, and then continue reading:

Graffiti is okay here. Mark it up. Underline *everything* that you recognize as *personal communication* from God to you as you read through the verse the first time. (Think of these lines as the swirls in that favorite ice cream.)

Allow time for everyone to underline the parts of Psalm 37:4 in their journals. *Note: It may vary from person to person.*

Next, read through those *underlined sections*, circling the words or phrases that are especially meaningful. (These would be the chunks in the ice cream.) It may be a glimpse of His character, a message of what He has done or what He wants you to do. It could be what He thinks of you. It may be an acknowledgement of a promise made or kept.

Students should work independently, circling as they feel led.

Now, write your response to God as a brief prayer letter using the circled words, and optionally the underlined sections. Since this is only one verse, not a chapter, we should be able to use both.

When all are ready, continue:

Read over what you wrote. Add any additional comments or requests that come to mind. Pray silently by reading your letter to God.

After every person has finished, ask for volunteers to read the letters that they wrote. Be sure not to call on anyone who does not offer to share. If you have a quiet bunch, you may either share your own, or you may read Sample Two in Section Six. Although it is ideal to have a few different comparisons, this is personal, and we want to maintain a comfortable environment. Encourage lightly without pushing. Every lesson is matched with a sample in Section Six, which can be used whenever necessary.

Top it off – Homework?

Homework for a prize! Give the following assignment and close in prayer.

- Read Sections Two through Five this week.
- Set up your Ongoing Prayer List (OPL) on a separate sheet of paper to use as a bookmark in your journal.
- Finish listing general prayer topics inside the cover of your journal or on your OPL according to the day of the week when you will regularly pray for them.

Jeri Daniel

DAY TWO

Set up...

Ensure that each student has what is needed for the lesson. By now, each one should have a Bible to write in, a journal, and a pen. Remember to have a Bible Dictionary, a study Bible, or a standard dictionary. Optionally, you may have printed copies of Psalm 27 for those without Bibles. (BibleGateway.com)

Before the students arrive, write this journal entry on the board:

(Date) Journal

- *Opening prayer*
- *OPL*
- *SCRIPTURE* – **Psalm 27**

Pay with prizes...

No matter what the age or stage, quickly pass out a prize to those who did their homework. Here are some prize ideas which you may use each week:

- A variety of pens can be purchased very inexpensively. Give one to each student who completed their weekly homework assignment.
- Gum is also inexpensive and comes in sugar free!
- Of course, there is always candy.
- Local restaurants often will donate ice cream coupons. All you have to do is ask.
- Be creative, but keep it simple.

Start with prayer…

Ask the Holy Spirit to guide the lesson and bring understanding. Pray that only the words which are meant to be spoken will be said, according to God's perfect will. Pray for the members of the group; God has each one there for a particular purpose. Pray that He will be glorified by the lesson.

Settle in…

Ice breaker game: Ice cream themed "Sit down if…" Everyone stands up to begin. You can play this twice, if time allows. For the first round, the Teacher reads through these statements, and the students sit down if it applies. The last one standing wins. He or she may get a prize *or* get to repeat the game, reading from the bottom of the list up.

Sit down if…

- Plain vanilla is your favorite ice cream.
- You like any plain ice cream better than with stuff in it.
- You don't like nuts in your ice cream.
- You don't like fruit flavored ice cream.
- You eat ice cream at least once a week.
- You don't like any kinds of swirls in your ice cream.
- You would rather go out for ice cream than have it at home.
- You like peanut butter in your ice cream.
- You like chocolate in your ice cream.
- You do not consider chocolate syrup and fudge swirls to be equal.

Subjects for prayers...

See if anyone has thought up any new topics that others may wish to add to their OPL (Ongoing Prayer Lists).

Super easy seatwork...

Each student should copy the sample journal entry from the white board onto the next, fresh journal page.

Savor the Savior together...

The group will share feedback from having read all of Section Four, "Questions and Answers" together. There are nine questions. Have one person read the question, and then a different person read the answer. *Note: The last answer reviews all that has been taught.*

Tune in to Teacher-Talk...

Teacher, read this aloud to the class:

Today's passage of Scripture is much longer than the first one that we did. We are actually going to conquer the whole chapter of Psalm 27 today. Remember, it is personal from God to you. Why is God telling you what He is telling you? Just think about it as you read and underline *everything* that you recognize as *personal communication* from God to you. (Think of these lines as the swirls in that favorite ice cream.)

Allow time for everyone to underline in their Bibles.

Next, read through only those *underlined sections*, circling the words or phrases that are especially meaningful. (These would be the chunks in the ice cream.) It may be a glimpse of

Who He is, a message of what He has done or what He wants you to do. It could be what He thinks of you. It may be an acknowledgement of a promise made or kept.

Students should work independently.

Now, write your response to God as a brief prayer letter using the circled words, and optionally the underlined sections.

When all are ready, continue:

Read over what you wrote. Add any additional comments or requests that come to mind. Pray silently by reading your letter to God.

After every person has finished, ask for volunteers to read the letters that they wrote. Be sure not to call on anyone who does not offer to share. If you have a quiet bunch, you may either share your own, or you may read Sample Three in Section Six. Although it is ideal to have a few different comparisons, this is personal and we want to maintain a comfortable environment. Encourage lightly without pushing. Every lesson is matched with a sample in Section Six, which can be used whenever necessary.

Top it off – Homework?

Homework for a prize! Give the following assignment and close in prayer.

- Complete any unfinished homework from last week.
- Review any portion of <u>Savor the Savior</u> as needed.
- Update your Ongoing Prayer List (OPL).

- Strive to find at least 20 minutes each day this week to pray, read the Bible, and record the prayer type and the Scripture address in your journal. Decide how many verses you will aim to read each day and stick with it.
- BONUS: Apply the complete <u>Savor the Savior</u> method for at least three days this week.

Savor the Savior

DAY THREE

Set up...

Ensure that each student has what is needed for the lesson. By now, each one should have a Bible to write in, a journal, and a pen. Remember to have a Bible Dictionary, a study Bible, or a standard dictionary. Optionally, you may have printed copies of Joshua 10:1-15 for those without Bibles. (BibleGateway.com)

Before the students arrive, write this journal entry on the board:

(Date) Journal

- *Opening prayer*
- *OPL*
- <u>*SCRIPTURE*</u> *– Joshua 10:1-15*

Pay with prizes...

No matter what the age or stage, quickly pass out a prize to those who did their homework. *(See Day Two for prize details.)*

Start with prayer...

Ask the Holy Spirit to guide the lesson and bring understanding. Pray that only the words which are meant to be spoken will be said, according to God's perfect will. Pray for the members of the group; God has each one there for a particular purpose. Pray that He will be glorified by the lesson.

Settle in...

Play the ice breaker game: "Don't say 'ice cream.'" This can be done as a group or in smaller groups of two or three. One person is the worker, who is to ask the customers how they would like their ice cream served. The customers must then answer as creatively as possible, but no one can say the actual word, "ice cream" or they are out. Set a timer for one minute rounds.

Subjects for prayers...

See if anyone has thought up any new topics that others may wish to add to their OPL (Ongoing Prayer Lists).

Super easy seatwork...

Each student should copy the sample journal entry from the white board onto the next, fresh journal page.

Savor the Savior together...

From Section Four, "Questions and Answers," have students say only the bold words from each bullet point in the last answer. Write these on the board, and see how quickly and clearly six people can each say one of these in order around the room without fumbling the words:

- **Pray**
- **Read**, underlining
- **Skim**, circling
- **Write** *to God*
- **Read**, Add
- **Close**

Tune in to Teacher-Talk...

Teacher, read this aloud to the class:

Today's passage of Scripture, Joshua 10:1-15, is very different from the second one that we did. Today we are going to do a portion of an Old Testament story, which may seem a bit more difficult to apply. It is still personal from God to you. Why is God telling you what He is telling you? Think about it as you read and underline *everything* that you recognize as *personal communication* from God to you. (Think of these lines as the swirls in that favorite ice cream.)

Allow time for everyone to underline in their Bibles.

Next, read through only those *underlined sections*, circling the words or phrases that are especially meaningful. (These would be the chunks in the ice cream.) It may be a glimpse of Who He is, a message of what He has done or what He wants you to do. It could be what He thinks of you. It may be an acknowledgement of a promise made or kept.

Students should work independently.

Now, write your response to God in your journal as a brief prayer letter using the circled words, and optionally the underlined sections.

When all are ready, continue:

Read over what you wrote. Add any additional comments or requests that come to mind. Pray silently by reading your letter to God.

After every person has finished, ask for volunteers to read the letters that they wrote. Be sure not to call on anyone who does not offer to share. If you have a quiet bunch, you may either share your own, or you may read Sample Four in Section Six. Although it is ideal to have a few different comparisons, this is personal and we want to maintain a comfortable environment. Encourage lightly without pushing. Every lesson is matched with a sample in Section Six, which can be used whenever necessary.

Top it off – Homework?

Homework for a prize! Give the following assignment and close in prayer.

- Complete any unfinished homework from previous weeks.
- Review any portion of <u>Savor the Savior</u> as needed.
- Update your Ongoing Prayer List (OPL).
- Strive to find at least 20 minutes each day this week to pray, read the Bible, and record the prayer type and the Scripture address in your journal. Decide how many verses you will aim to read each day and stick with it.
- Apply the complete <u>Savor the Savior</u> method for at least five days this week.

Savor the Savior

DAY FOUR

Set up...

Ensure that each student has what is needed for the lesson. By now, each one should have a Bible to write in, a journal, and a pen. Remember to have a Bible Dictionary, a study Bible, or a standard dictionary. Optionally, you may have printed copies of Ephesians 4:29-5:2 for those without Bibles. (BibleGateway.com)

Before the students arrive, write this journal entry on the board:

(Date) Journal

- *Opening prayer & OPL*
- *SCRIPTURE – **Ephesians 4:29-5:2***

Pay with prizes...

No matter what the age or stage, quickly pass out a prize to those who did their homework. *(See Day Two for prize details.)*

Start with prayer...

Ask the Holy Spirit to guide the lesson and bring understanding. Pray that only the words which are meant to be spoken will be said, according to God's perfect will. Pray for the members of the group; God has each one there for a particular purpose. Pray that He will be glorified by the lesson.

Settle in...

Ask any or all of these questions, either allowing everyone to answer the same one, or taking turns with different questions.

Would you rather...

- Always choose the ice cream flavor for everyone else around you, but never get to eat ice cream yourself, or get to eat ice cream, but never get to choose the flavor?
- Never eat ice cream for the rest of your life, or have to eat ice cream with every meal for the rest of your life?
- Eat ice cream lying down or standing on one foot?

Or for those who want to go a bit sillier...

Would you rather...

- Soak your feet in soft ice cream for 30 minutes, or place a scoop of hard ice cream under each arm pit for 3 minutes?
- Eat ice cream topped with lint or topped with dead ants?
- Would you rather eat a turkey stuffed with ice cream, or ice cream topped with turkey?

You may let students come up with their own, but set the limits right up front.

Subjects for prayers...

See if anyone has thought up any new topics that others may wish to add to their OPL (Ongoing Prayer Lists).

Super easy seatwork...

Each student should copy the sample journal entry from the white board onto the next, fresh journal page.

Savor the Savior together...

Say each word, and ask for volunteers to explain how it fits into the Savor the Savior method:

- Pray
- Underline
- Circle
- Write
- Read
- Add
- Close

Tune in to Teacher-Talk...

Teacher, read this aloud to the class:

Today you will learn an abbreviated method in order to still fit in prayer, Bible study, and journaling on days when time is extremely limited. This is not intended to replace regular love letters to God. It will, however, equip you with the ability to invest quality time, even when the quantity is lacking.

Ephesians 4:29-5:2 is packed with personal applications from God to us. Ask yourself, "Why is God telling me this?" Think about it as you read and underline *everything* that you recognize as *personal communication* from God to you. (Think of these lines as the swirls in that favorite ice cream.)

Allow time for everyone to underline in their Bibles.

Next, read through only those *underlined sections*, circling the words or phrases that are especially meaningful. (These would be the chunks in the ice cream.) It may be a glimpse of Who He is, a message of what He has done or what He wants you to do. It could be what He thinks of you. It may be an acknowledgement of a promise made or kept.

Students should work independently.

Now, this is where it is different. *List the circled words only,* **separating them with commas.**

When all are ready, continue:

Read over what you wrote. Add any additional words, comments, or requests that come to mind. Pray silently by reading your list to God.

After every person has finished, ask for volunteers to read the lists that they wrote. Be sure not to call on anyone who does not offer to share. If you have a quiet bunch, you may either share your own, or you may read Sample Five in Section Six. Although it is ideal to have a few different comparisons, this is personal and we want to maintain a comfortable environment. Encourage lightly without pushing. Every lesson is matched with a sample in Section Six, which can be used whenever necessary.

Top it off – Homework?

Give the following assignment, and read the "Teacher's Closure" on the next page aloud. Close in prayer.

- Complete any unfinished homework from previous weeks.
- Review any portion of Savor the Savior as needed.

- Update your Ongoing Prayer List (OPL).
- Strive to find at least 20 minutes each day this week to pray, read the Bible, and record the prayer type and the Scripture address in your journal. Decide how many verses you will aim to read each day and stick with it.
- Apply the complete Savor the Savior method for six days this week.
- *CHALLENGE:* Find an accountability partner of the same gender, to help you to consistently make it 21 days in a row without skipping time alone with the Lord. Count the days in your journal to keep track. Ask for prayer to complete this goal to develop a habit for life.

Teacher's Closure

(From the Conclusion at the end of Section Three)

Teacher, read this aloud to the class:

You did it! Listen to these verses about spiritual growth and maturity:

> *Anyone who lives on milk, being still an infant, is not acquainted with the teaching about righteousness. But solid food is for the mature, who by constant use have trained themselves to distinguish good from evil.*
> Hebrews 5:13-14

> *Taste and see that the LORD is good; blessed is the man who takes refuge in him.*
> Psalm 34:8

Jeri Daniel

May you move from living on "milk" to digesting the "solid food" of His Word each and every day. *Taste and see that the Lord is good!* Savor the Savior!

Jeri Daniel is available for speaking engagements and personal appearances. For more information contact:

Jeri Daniel
C/O Advantage Books
PO Box 160847
Altamonte Springs, FL 32716

Jeri@knowhisway.org

Please visit the author's website at:
www.knowhisway.org

To purchase additional copies of this book or other books published by Advantage Books call our toll free order number at: 1-888-383-3110 (Book Orders Only)
or visit our bookstore website at:www.advbookstore.com

Longwood, Florida, USA
"we bring dreams to life"™
www.advbooks.com

www.ingramcontent.com/pod-product-compliance
Lightning Source LLC
Chambersburg PA
CBHW032210040426
42449CB00005B/521